Boy with Flowers

Boy with Flowers

Ely Shipley

Barrow Street Press
New York City

Designed by Robert Drummond

Published by Barrow Street Press
Distributed by:
      Barrow Street
      P.O. Box 1831
      Murray Hill Station
      New York, NY 10156

First Edition

Library of Congress control number: 2008902476

ISBN 978-0-9728302-8-7

for my given and my chosen
families

CONTENTS

3.

1.

After the Carnival

It's night. Each of us wears

a mask. I am
the pig, and you
the hawk. Children hide,

folding into their mothers'
skirts, as we kiss

each other and sometimes
them. Beak and snout smear

spread-open lines of red
lipstick. We smother

each with snorts and caws, our skin
pressing in the rubber
glued between us, heat

and sweat making it hard
to breathe, breathe–

because inside your chest, a rocket
explodes. Because

at thirteen, a high school boy
held your head
under water at Lytle Creek. Inside

you couldn't swim
so clutched his neck, his arm
until he lifted

your face, smashing his face
into your mouth, sucking

your breath. On the ride home
you puked in the back
of his truck, where his dog

growled when you bit
your fist or wiped

your chin. And you were shivering
the way you are now, pressed

between shadows that keep shifting
beneath fireworks falling

all around us, like feathers
and blood from a shot bird.

Roll of Dimes

He removed the blade
from an old razor for me

and taught me *smooth
downward strokes.* Did I go

with him to work that day, or
an Angel's game? Did I

wear a dress and argue I should
wear a tie like him, or my jersey and cap? Was I already

in school, and did I tell him what I'd learned
from other kids? Words

I didn't understand, got slapped for
saying in the grocery store

to my brother? Did I tell him
who I fought each day at recess

when they spit on me or hit me
first, in the back of the head

and hard? I must have,
I'm sure of it now. Because I remember him

placing a roll of dimes
in my tiny hand, *wrap*

your fist around it, he said, *now
hit my hand, punch it*

like you're the Champ. And I felt
the weight of it

driving my fist into his palm
which swelled up

red and I imagined a sting,
while my own fingers got crushed

over and over again, between
all I held and wanted

to push away.

Encounter

In shop windows, torsos
of mannequins, and a cricket
nests in the chest of one.

It is not a heart, but longs for
its other. Exhaling

mist, I push away
from this glass, feel
my sex is a sea

shell, its slug, small
mollusk, shrinking into its own

wetness or elongating into
a hardness. I think of the male sea

horse, carrying the female's
eggs, birthing thousands
of fry, a semenlike spray–

out and away with no
receptacle, except this

world, submerged. And so
the self is multiplied. Once

home, I see
my face through the fogged

bathroom mirror, at the bottom
of a teacup, inside polished
silver, or at the bulbous end

of a long-stem wineglass, where
my lip meets its and I remember

that it has been made
from blown glass,

the shape of someone's
breath, held.

A Farmhouse

Rain-stained redwood and eggshell in the hay.
I wanted, finally,

to shake a stranger's hands, simply
without my hands

shaking. Some birds flit
over water, kissing their reflections

before they dive in for a slender fish, a flash of

silver. And here, moss gathered
along chimneys, nearly

glowing in the fog. I could hardly lift
my arm to rest it

at the small of your back. And only went on

to imagine
nothing more than touching

your hair, neither the color
of rust nor ash, but snow, one thick
ribbon of winter, cold in my palm,

a place I once breathed
myself a warm breath.

Boy with Flowers

My aunt loved me, asked me:
will you be the flower
girl at my wedding? But I'm not
a girl, I argued, and she persuaded me:
you'll get to throw rose petals

onto the aisle, walk before me, both of us
crushing them beneath our feet, my gown
dragging over them. I agreed. I wanted
nothing but chivalry.

At the church, my mother and I
waited in the small room. She brushed
my aunt's hair until the dress arrived.
Isn't it beautiful? And I agreed until they tried
to put me in it. I'd seen my father

and uncle earlier, standing in a circle
of other men, smoke hovering over their heads, a halo
and their voices kind, quiet, and deep. I told my aunt –
I want to wear a suit like them! She promised

if I wore the dress I could wear anything
I wanted after: army pants, a sheriff
badge, cowboy hat, and pistols. My mother shot her
a look in the mirror where we posed, both of them
angelic in white, and me, not yet

dressed. Today I wake from another dream
in which I have a beard, no breasts
and am about to go skinny-dipping
on a foreign beach with four other men.

I'm afraid to undress, won't take off my shorts,
so they grab me, one at each ankle, the other two
by each wrist. I am a starfish hardening.
The sun hovers above, a hot
mirror where I search for my reflection.

I close my eyes. It's too intense. The light
where my lover is tracing fingertips
around two long incisions in my chest. Each sewn tight
with stitches, each a naked stem, flaring with thorns.

Balloons

With each square
dream, I am suddenly home-
sick, remembering
the first girl I loved: the warmth of her
breath through the sleeve of her
throat: my hand held there to take
her pulse in science class. It had been
winter, and cold—I wanted her

breathing as my own. Now each canvas is
a lung hung in a single body, exhaling
green to red, blue to gold. She bends
over me, washes my hair in our kitchen
cluttered with brushes. Dried paint
loosens, streaks down
the sink, just past my face
and eyes, filling
up with color.

Army Tattoos

They said he liked to gamble, called him
a lucky winner. He bet on horses, liked to

lie on his belly before
a TV, drinking a glass

of bourbon or smoking cigars, thick
smoke between his lips, black as the rims

of those spectacles sliding off
his sweating face. Between commercials,

he'd tell stories—one
about Job, the other a Japanese

prison camp, where he forced himself
to eat in the shadows the maggots

hiding in the rice. I understood
and I didn't. I was ten, played barefoot

in the backyard desert, drank sun tea
with lemon, took naps in the patch of grass

we kept trying to grow. I'd wake up frightened
that snakes or scorpion babies had

crept into my ears. And later I'd sneak
and spy the shed skin, collected in jars, lining

the garage shelves. Then, inside the house
the hearts that hung purple and beatless

from the living room mantle, with so many other
medals and photos. With my magic marker, I'd trace

onto myself those green dreams
of the skull, the black

cat, the number thirteen, tattoos
that wrapped around each wrist and forearm.

Hidden in the pantry, I'd draw myself
out of that dark, camouflage my skin as his.

fever & halo

That August someone burned
inside a neighboring house. The arsonist
left a black glove in our garden
and a wig on the street. Limp
scalp. That night I dreamed

a white goat gorged itself
on cocoa beans and the rare drizzle of rain
woke me. My sheets were stained
with blood. My mother said
You're no longer

      a girl. Soon after, I buried

the picture of a boy I'd drawn
in the small shade of a yucca. I prayed for
nearby fire ants to eat
his face from the page. Perhaps they would

grow into a gnarled desert
tree. One might sprout
wings, shed seed shells
into the air above my bed, steam

cooing in the heat, a mirage
heard. A heavy black cello
hums overhead.

Inertia

In a room at dusk, my father's hands
unfold as sails

caught in wind. He tells me
of the Alzheimer brain,

the autopsy he saw on TV—
all deterioration, holes eating through,
a piece of coral. My oma sits behind

a window somewhere in Montana,
watches snowflakes accumulate,
blanket earth. She is

wrapped in a shawl she crocheted long before
her hands knotted up, arthritic, into ropes
pulled down by invisible

anchors. Is it a dream she lives
inside now? That one with the German boys, who
turned her sled, made her fall,
when she was a girl? She never cried

but pushed one into the freezing
pond, ran home, told no one. This story
she has told me again and again,

my whole life. Hers will look like coral
one day too, my father says. We both know
this description is far

too beautiful. But knowing makes us
feel safe. Knowing, for example,

that because the roller coaster goes fast enough,
its passengers won't fall out

even as it turns them
upside-down through its loops.

Do people cry out
not because they're afraid

to fall, but because
they delight

in their safety and know
they won't?

Magnolia

In the cul-de-sac shaded
by trees, Marissa and I
played all summer where magnolias
hung, hands withering over us
as we wove

between them. In her backyard
we circled the empty,
dirty pool where petals and leaves
floated, where insects waded. We came to a shed
hidden in the back

corner of her yard; jars held pale, slick
shapes, cylindrical and bulbed, only
later I learned were preserved
vegetables. Marissa swore they were

testicles and a penis, and when I didn't believe her, no—
they were fingers, eyes, and tongues
her stepfather collected, who later that day
I met by mistake. He'd come home early,

liquor on his breath, speaking
slowly, quietly, and only
in Spanish, though I was also in that congested
room where every curtain was
closed and the air thick

with heat, whispering. And Marissa's face
stiffening into a mask, glazed
with sweat, her eyes cast
down as he punched

the air, each syllable a balled-up
fist. Marissa told me then
I wasn't allowed inside her
house anymore. Outside, as if
to apologize, she picked me

a magnolia blossom. And I carried it
carefully in my sweating
hands, not yet understanding
by the time I got home

the petals would no longer be
white but darkening everywhere
they'd been touched.

2.

In the Film

A woman tells
her therapist she hears
rabbits live their whole lives
without a noise
until killed, then scream,

and sound almost human.
There is no music, only
the clatter of her speech,
which ricochets through my head
while something lodges

in my throat, sharp
as a stone shot from
the heart's sling. Inside

the theater, my breath
quickens. I am sliding
backward, trying to climb

a barbed-wire fence
when I was ten. Tangled up,
I wanted to yell for help.
I'd been playing war
with a boy and winning

until I launched a rock
so high I couldn't tell where it would land.
It seemed to get lost

in the sun, to become the sun
for a moment, then
fall, striking his skull. A line

of red divided his face. I ran,
never saw him again. The woman
in the movie falls

in love but still feels
trapped. I know because
one night she makes love in the choir
loft of an abandoned church. The roof

seems as though it is peeled
open and the camera
closes in so I can look

down on her. It begins to rain,
and when she comes
the noise she makes, breathing heavily

into the man's hair, which is long and sways
like a curtain back and forth across his face,
sounds like singing.

hair & dream

1.
Our warm home, snow
melting in my hair. Glancing

myself in the mirror, *glass
beads.* I tell you:

we swam in a fountain
where minnows sang, *silver*

violins. Summer. Now you are
taking off my coat, towel-

drying my hair.

2.
Do you hear it growing
while I sleep? Sometimes
tips burrow into earth. With nothing
to cut it, I ask you to help me

chew it away, and here
I only see myself in a glass. I look
lonely and don't

speak. How
quiet hair is, and how it goes on for so long,
even after someone.

Glass

A disco ball gleams, an eye
of God, and I'm reflected
thousands of times, tiny
in squares until I can't breathe,

drowning in the sounds of bass
I mistake for my heart. The other dancers—
my shadows, come closer to, then farther
from me, sprayed out in the strobe
lights, pressing me in and out of two

times, two worlds. My face I remember
from this morning behind a fog of
breath in the bathroom
mirror, and the bar-

tender, who said, *It's not the heart
I'm after,* his eyes following another
man on his way out. In this club I see
myself upside down inside a woman's

glass. I sit next to her and she holds me
between her fingers, then her lips. She tilts
me back with her head, but I'm never quite right

side up. Instead, I just disappear
somewhere inside her.

Horizon Line

All contour, the neck, the terra-cotta skin
stitched tight, the place my aunt describes
to children, *where,* she says, *I was torn*

open by sharks, or *forced at knife-point*
to walk the plank.
But really it was that

glaze of white, to her a sudden cloud
or stallion, galloping off the page of a novel,
some story–
a car crashed into hers, simply

gliding surreal and slow as a childhood
paper plane crumpling. One engine locked into
another, into breastbone, the heart

brick struck by a hammer. She was
cloaked in that red, inside out, her hair
a web around her face, eyelashes and glass, spittle
and metal entwined. But I only hear this

in the after, the shade
of a tree on a New England lawn,
early spring. I feel as if
I am inside that car, I am that car, and I am

drifting into her
as if into a box. I hang here, small
sphere orbiting inside this

planetarium. I am heady with the weight of how
fragile we are, how disembodied, then composed. Here
is where the sun hides, a voice which speaks from beyond

my aunt's perforated throat. It is the map to a place
I will never enter but wish to
trail with my fingers, read the Braille
of her, follow

this story as the needle that once
reassembled her dug deep—little silver
diver plunging into water, then

up for air, sewing itself between two
worlds, here and there, me
and her, to stitch

all that can only be
seamless in the dark.

Shroud

She lived in the projects
as a child, scared
of the strange woman
who was always hidden

under long sleeves and skirts—
shrouded in mystery my mother
had said. She'd try to sleep
each night, fantasizing
that the woman had arrived

from a carnival, was really
covered head to toe in tattoos,
although she never knew
for certain. As a child I, too,
dreamed about the woman, how I wanted

stories painted here
into my body. I would never
undress, but even now my veins feel etched

through the muscles
of my heart and arms,
kept safe

from the air, like the silent
fish swimming deep
inside rivers through caves
without needing

eyes to see. Think of how gently
rain must have fallen
into the open

stare of my mother. How color
must have blossomed
from its blue root.

Breath

As if a lullaby, the city hums
electronically through evening, the sky
a mist, ballooning with light. The sound,
my neighbor's late-night cough is the only thing

that pulls me back to my simple room, walls
painted with shadows, black, and then a car's
headlights washing over. Or the deeper scars
cut there, dried leaves rattled in wind, some

sacred instrument from another time
or country. I only imagine this because I want
escape. My shirt opened,
you used to draw invisibly across my chest

with your fingers, the outlines of words, letters,
skeletons of things. You pasted kisses inside
each of my hands, and now, when I close
my eyes, a music box starts up and my breath

is that lonely ballerina, spiraling
faster before her circular mirror. And she sees
nothing, because it is dark
or because her eyes are only eyes

painted across a face. Yet for a moment
I swear I hear her sing
over the music, the city, my pulse—
but it's only the high-pitched, slow churning

of her feet, that wood carved tightly
around a metal spring, the way
the whole world turns and folds
around its invisible axis.

Sent

Unlike the teenage boy who sends
love letters one summer, nothing written on them
but *Love*—I only want to write you

about the fountain I photographed
last summer in the rain. Behind white lines
strumming down, still figures blur under black
umbrellas. A bicycle's spokes glisten
in the foreground—or the way today,
writing this, my coffee has turned cold.
It is not enough to tell you

I miss you. Understand I also miss
myself. The voice singing now
from the radio belongs to a dead woman, & the clouds
have nothing to say to me. Every Sunday

I walk to the cemetery to look at the flowers
dying against the headstones. Once
I saw a young girl bend toward a red
carnation, as if its scent were sweeter
there. When she left, I couldn't bring myself

to do the same. Today I will walk to Echo Park
to listen to the man who presses himself

against his cart of ice cream, & rings
a bell. Maybe a woman dozing on her balcony
will lift herself & call to her small son, let go

a handful of dimes, shimmering down
against the shore at our feet.

Fountain

Near a garden, I hear singing.
Between buildings, an old woman folds
paper bags into squares, tiling a shopping cart.
I think, *little brick house.* I've been
dreaming nearly every night of such houses.
Some have been gutted and most are haunted.
I wander from room to room and in one find
my mother's heart, which looks to me like the cartilage
of a shark I saw as a child on a field trip to the Museum
of Natural History. I begin to believe the heart is covered
by shell. It looks as if it is embedded with pearls
or teeth. My mother must have left it by mistake, here
on a shelf. I want to lift it to my ear and listen to its beating.
I'm afraid to touch it, afraid I'll hear only silence,
and the silence will carry me into its sea. I could drown in this
love for my mother. Inside the garden, a stone
fountain floats, from which water pours endlessly
from the mouths of fish and gods.

City of Angels

your skin was sheathed in
       cracked glass. Little egg,
       little pupa, pockmarked
       moon we'd been

       waiting for you to hatch

       light-scaled wings, music
       engraved in them. Your voice
       volcanic. All summer

       erupted. Fourth
       of. Ash after. You melt
       what you touch. Me,

       cool
       under your breath.

*

April in Little Tokyo.
Rain and green tea

ice cream. Foggy lights in a sky
scraper. Your small hip

in my hand. We waltzed slipperlike
ninja-shoed

through exhibitions of

bloody thighs, fur
pie, afros, and mascara-

streaked cheeks. Later, in the dank

*

summer of Echo Park, we listened
to the water lap

against the lotus
leaves. The sounds of

men's bodies
rustling inside bushes, as if

to get out.

Night around Me

In a parking lot in L.A., ice-cream
trucks sleep with their nursery rhymes
turned silent, near houses

whose barred windows
guard those asleep
inside. Nearby

dyke clubs open; the Pinkbox,
Milk; and from the Meow
Mix, music seeps, spills out

into the street, and the smog
feels lower because of the city's light
pollution. I take it

through my mouth and skin. Inside
spotlights glint off glasses
of beer, and I'm

drowsing in the haze and fuzz
of electric guitars, held by girls
with short-cropped hair and tiny

bow ties. Between songs, the clink
of pool cues against balls pulses
as metronomes, and all sounds move

deeper in through my chest and arms,
thighs, and groin. Later, between those
parked trucks, easy as breath, my girl knows

I can see myself inside her. Inside her
eyes, where she watches me and I become
silhouetted and small, simple

as the shadow of a tear, a burnt-out
matchstick, candlewick,
thorn, a thorn I feel

bite into my lip when she kisses me
with her teeth. And her eyes
close around me.

A Wave

Her hand
on my back, a warped record turning silently under the needle,
beneath pressure. Patience.

Our milky shadow shaped like a door.

The click of the key in the lock, turning again, and again.

Then, the body of the bird against the glass. A single feather
that fluttered

there, after. We remember
the music. Trumpets once golden

birds siphoning secrets from the lungs of men.

I say, try, tuck your breath
under its wing.

Only the stiff black branch of night
and clouds, held up
by a draft. I swear I hear

roots burrow into frozen earth. The sound of
ice cracking. What

will grow here? Come to bed now, sleep,

I say. I am wilting.
From outside I feel as if

a great wave is rushing
toward us. It arrives
and breaks

over us
soft confetti.

After Our Fight

She disappears inside the movie theater. The show is
a hand of lightning reaching through
windows and turning everything to glass. The windows are only
air with thin curtains, but look like waterfalls. She said everything
will be beautiful, exposed. Out on the street

I think and wait with hands in pockets, so imagine
I'm inside that movie and she's watching me. I'm a man
lying on a bed. I light a cigarette and toss the match
at a window. Curtains flame into hands. They crawl over
one another, black waves fanning out across the ceiling. I pretend

to sleep, and hope she'll worry about me. I pretend to dream
of stealing cars and spying on lovers, creeping on my belly across a hotel
parking lot, then jump a barbed-wire fence and run along the train
tracks. I'm a kid again and nearly forget

I'm burning for her. That's when the bull comes
charging after me and a flood of people. I grab onto
a window ledge, hoist myself up, half
expecting her hands to be there, pulling me awake, back

inside the burning, which must, by now, be a volcano.
But I'm only holding the bull's horns and know it's ridiculous
to think she'd save me, but I do, and I'm scared,
so let go.

3.

He lay down

with abandon. His eyes
dull marble, his shadow
a friend seeping

out from his head,
a sudden widow's

shawl. Next to him, a winter
branch. And inside, no one

to answer the phone. It goes on
ringing. Out on the lawn,

a flower's petals fall.
They are the color of twilight. And the neighbors

begin to turn on warm lamps
in living room windows, and stare down into their steaming
dinner plates, which are white as shells from the sea,

whose echoes they breathe and
fork onto their tongues. Night

came. A soft rain
began. Three misty halos

blurred the traffic light, blinking
the colors of Christmas
and insomnia.

He picked himself up. Climbed
the apartment stairs, reaching his fingers out
the whole way

to touch the doorknob,
the piano's keys. He did not press down

but cleared his throat, the sound of
an anchor ratcheting

across the sea floor.
He was humming a lullaby, and turning

pages from a calendar. He closed
the curtains. His hands

were small
children he thought were starving.
He looked at their bones and wished he knew
their names. What

would he call them? They were thin
strands of smoke he could coil

together. Was one the shadow
of the other? He thought he would have liked

to visit the mountains with them, to hold a single
pinecone in each of his palms, transferring
the heat of one hand to the other.

If heat were a seed, what would it grow?
Perhaps there would be

a waterfall, and someone
splashing there
under its veils.

Memory

When I was four, a man
selling flowers on an island in the center
of a city street leaned into my father's
car window and placed one in
my hair. More than petals, I remember

the dirt beneath his nails
as if he'd just pulled those flowers
from a garden, and for me only. My father
drove forward, his eyes
flashing quickly

in the rearview mirror. Pale
seeds, or tiny eggs left blind
in an abandoned nest. Tonight
the scent of burning sage

blossoms over the boulevard
and lip of shore. A man bundles
the dried leaves with colored thread: blue,
red, gold. His hands

are quick and open. And the smoke
touches me, brushes
through my hair its gray wing.

Reflexive

In my father's house are many mansions.
        —John 14:2

His hair so blond it was
nearly white. I never saw but imagine it

cascade around his crown. A laurel, a halo
his mother's hands ran through. Imagine

his white shepherd the neighbor
poisoned. My father leaning

against a barbed fence
near its body, a thick white

pelt in the middle of a desert,
whistling a dirge into the soft ears

of a once distant field

horse. Its nostrils unfurling
an audible

breath against his face,
as the diver feels himself shattering

into his reflection inside a
pool's translucent skin.

Man at a Bar

From the hearth's nest
of twigs and logs, smoke
coils up and a stranger
slouched over the bar
contemplates the separation

of spirit from the body. I know this
because the heart does break,
and the body can only
collapse around it. I think
of him as a child, just nearing
the age of loneliness, carving

his initials over and over
into an oak in the schoolyard,
an arrow through yet no heart
around them. But tonight
he squints, takes the last

drag from his cigarette
as it turns into a long finger
of broken ash. Deep in his lungs,
he cradles its smoke: flames

hatch open, fly
into a heaven. And rain
shatters from a sky
that has never ceased
to be immense.

Mirror

The violin a nest
catching fire. Each string
melts. The instrument's wood
an amber pool.

*

My pulse flares
white. The heart must be
light shot up
casting its net
over everything.

*

The glint on the gold of a childhood
trophy. The featureless
man propels himself
forward. Feet sealed
to the pedestal.

*

The moon in the lake I am
able to touch, or nearly.
The crescent, a pale
fish, a silk fan dropped
into black. My arm, half
gone, blurs the picture. The waves
soft and small. A moth's wings flutter
a powder against my face. I smear each
star with a finger. And the feeling is rain.

Six

The neck of the guitar stretches
out, every other fret painted with a sharp
dot or dash, flash after flash

of reflected light, marble or pearl, the shape
of a fingerprint, the measure of each
note trapped inside
the instrument's dark.

Outside, a hailstorm
and the sound of crumpled-
up grade-school exams once
smacking against

my skull, paper fists thrown angry
in torrents, and six-year-old
laughter that fell
all around me as I sat inside

a classroom, in a warm pool
of my own urine. I'd been ashamed
to go to the girls' room at recess,
because I was a boy,

they'd said. But the recess lady made me
stay away from the boys' room: You are
a girl. And later, my teacher: No,

no hall pass for the rest
of the year. So my body couldn't stop
secreting in class. Even my eyes and nose
seeped with the stuff. Out of control,

I heaved sobs between sharply phrased
taunts of what, what are you?
But tonight, I only want to be
the mouth

of a guitar, hollowed out
and bodiless
except for that balloon
of sound resonating invisibly

through air, and go on
pressing my fingers deeper in
to the neck, as if I could find
a shape inside

its voice as I choke
out its notes, its high-pitched
scream, its pop.

Through Walls

Think of the elephant who sleeps standing, a ghost
cradled in the curve of his swaying
trunk. I sweep snow

from my front porch, listen to the climbing
notes my neighbor sings. I hear *blood
stained . . . blackberry . . .* & *Argentina.* Maybe

he sings in Spanish. I close my eyes, press
myself against the cool white wall. Somewhere
an insect sleeps inside

an untouched piano key, the lip
of a still church bell, an old
radio that's been gutted & left

on my lawn. It fills with snow.
When spring comes I'll bring it inside, overflowing
with violets & silence.

Transgendered Teens on D.C. Street, August 12, 2002

for Stephanie Thomas and Ukea Davis

That night they lay
huddled as if in sleep
inside

a car. Corner
gas station. Out for cigarettes.
It looked as if

their heart—singular,
shared, and too big
for either chest, burst. Blood

at first sat in spots, buttons
sewn across a blouse, sudden
and undone. Each

shot more than
ten times
in the face. I believe
the undiscovered

assailant could not
bear their bodies
the way they must.
All their life

lived inside a ghetto within
a ghetto. If only I could be just
a passerby on their street, glancing
up at their brownstone porch, not

down at their shared
headstone, and listen

to a scrap of laughter
over traffic, heat, and what
they might have been

saying to each other
above the everyday and through
exhaled smoke.

Memorial

1.
At sixteen, driving a girl
across the desert inside my father's

'76 Chevy Monte Carlo, listening
to the distortion of its

radio, inhaling that heat
thick with dust, I passed
motels, Joshua and yucca
trees, cacti. All of my life

unfolding before me, no
mirage, and the lights of the city
dried up behind us.

2.
Inside the dim
kindergarten classroom, the old
film projector rattled, flashed—rackety
reel coiling, a voice
repeating. I turned back

to see its image
in a boy's glasses. Our eyes met.
We stared across that

room. Who could cut this invisible
thread? Someone turned on the light.
Next day, his sisters walked

across ten blocks of rain
to wake me from my sick
sleep, brought me a rose
he picked that morning.

Taking the flower, I thought
of him then, staring
all day at school
at my empty desk,

how that flower must have felt
inside his hand.

3.
Tonight the moon is a tin bell
silenced, its tongue wrapped
in gauze. It glitters dully, but only
if I tilt

my head just so.
A few hours ago, I slept
with someone. I can never know

whether I was loved, even
a little. And even
if I was, this sadness

welling up in me won't
stop. How
can the night ever be
brighter?

4.
Somewhere a young boy
pushes blazing lanterns
out over black water

to remember his dead. He holds
a small blue flame, carries it

from candlewick to
candlewick, then back
to his lips, blows it out, watches

a pale thread
unravel, disappear.

Waves

Outside a branch bends. No rain or sun
beats down on it. A father
rips it from the trunk, tears into the skin

of his small son, whose chest is pressed
into his bed, as if it were time

to pray, time to sleep, and this
is what the boy thinks of:

the blond grass on the hillside
burning and rolling
downward. He wants to follow

with his feet bare in the hot
ash, which clings to him
until his skin is the color of
smoke, the sky, and the strange

sea before a storm I once saw
at the south end of England
just before it thrashed

a boat to pieces. The next day it was
a pile of bones, the frame a rib
cage in which a child crouched

to play, filling his red
bucket with sea anemones and shells,
in that land where it is not uncommon

to see a man wearing a single golden
hoop in one ear, which guarantees him
a proper burial should he die
while out to sea.

Dear C.—

The side of your house peeled open.
Our friends rowed up in small boats
with lanterns, and waited for you to open your curtains, red
and flecked with gold. I thought of your tongue
and your tooth, your gift horse tattoo. Everyone
expected you to sing karaoke. But you were blowing
some old guy inside the dragon-swing ride
on the pier outside our favorite bar. The sound of its piano
drifting out over the water must have made you want
to die. When he left he pressed a crumpled bill
into your fist. You held it like a flower, then tossed it
into the waves. I swam beneath you
to catch it. That's when the curtain lifted
and your room was a sail filling with light.
We could see your face there, a movie, crying.
But no one could hear you. It started to rain.
Everyone opened their umbrellas and watched
until the wind carried you away.

Song

Hotel in the rain & the shelter
of palm trees. On the other side

of this street, a girl sings
along the shore. Her voice pulls me out

as if I were an endless chain
of colored scarves

unfolding from the magician's sleeve,
the heart sudden & unclenched.

Once I was a child burning
a leaf through a magnifying glass,

then tracing the veins
of my oma's hands.

I did as I was told, bringing the spring
in from the snow. Holding

a yellow primrose in my palm
I promised to love her

forever. Now I only want
to see her face, and so

follow her voice, with my eyes
closed, into the sea,

where I listen
with my hair

tangled in the coral,
& my feet planted

in the air above me.

Goya: Self-Portrait

Dear friend,
I'm sleeping inside

a desert where first I witness
stars—each man
in his own tent burning

a single oil lantern. And my own skull,
I realize, holds a flame, a kind of whisper I make
sense of by tracing

a brush across the jawline, the nostril,
and eye pit. How heavy are the beakless

parrots on my shoulders, waking
to imitate my breathing with their expanding
feathers. And don't forget the wingless

owl, who nests and then sobs from inside
my throat and chest because he hasn't

the answer, nothing
to expose. And now the light is

only a gauze, hanging inside so many
strange faces, like the face I have

seen passing every day
before my own mirror, clear

now as water in a glass, sincere
as the eye that sees itself.

Etymology

Strange that you'd let me
give birth
to my own body

even though I know I've always been
a boy, moving
toward what? Manhood? A constant

puberty? I could replace my menses
with a thick needle
filled with your fluid, thrust every

two weeks the rest of my life
into my thigh. And I think
of the six days of creation before

God rested, because I too am tired
and because my voice, would it suddenly be
God-like to me, thundering,

waking in a deep vibrato as if from atop
a mountain, maybe Olympus, maybe
a lightning bolt shot sharp

through my heart because I am
startled, scared, delighted?
You are the Magnetic

Fields, Elvis, and molasses, the first time
I heard Nina Simone sing, unsure of her
and my own sex at age 13. You are

an eighteen-wheeler ripping through
a hailstorm, the umpire breathing
over the catcher's shoulder until

the ball burns into the mitt
and there is the deep growl
ascending, *Strike one!*

And I am struck
hard by the beauty of you. I am
again an eight-year-old boy, simply

admiring a tree in the schoolyard, my only
friend who lifts me
and lifts me so that I can pick

its single spring
flower, the lowest one, maybe
for my mother, maybe my father—

but end up placing it inside
my first and only dictionary, a gift
from my father on the first day

of that school year. And later
when it has dried, wilted, I
remove it. Only a stain left, small

shadow, the handprint of
a child
quieting the words.

Acknowledgments

Thanks to the editors of the following publications in which these poems, some in different forms, originally appeared:

Barrow Street: "Sent," "Fountain," "After Our Fight"
Bloom: "Magnolia"
Diagram: "Horizon Line"
Florida Review: "Army Tattoos"
Greensboro Review: "Dear C.—"
Gulf Coast: "Reflexive"
Hayden's Ferry Review: "Roll of Dimes," "Six"
LTTR: "After the Carnival"
North American Review: "Breath," "Goya: Self-Portrait"
Painted Bride Quarterly (#77 online & print annual): "Glass"
Phoebe: "Inertia"
Prairie Schooner: "Boy with Flowers," "Etymology," "Memory," "Night Around Me"
The Western Humanities Review: "Encounter," "hair & dream," "In the Film," "Song," "Through Walls"
Willow Springs: "Man at a Bar"
"Shroud" appeared in the collection *Hard Travelin' and Still Havin' a Good Time: The Johnston Center 1979-2004,* Trafford Press, February 2004.

Thanks also to *Prairie Schooner* and Hilda Raz for the 2006 Virginia Faulkner Award, and to *The Western Humanities Review* and Edward Hirsch for the 2006 Utah Writer's Award. Special thanks to the editors of *Barrow Street,* especially Peter Covino; and gratitude to Carl Phillips for selecting this book.

Gratitude, also, to Rebecca Bednarz, Esther Lee, Shira Dentz, and the writing community at Utah for your friendship and kind attention to initial drafts of these poems, and to my teachers, Sandy Alps, Joy Manesiotis, Ralph Angel, Marianne Boruch, Donald Platt, Siobhan Somerville, Jacqueline Osherow, Paisley Rekdal, and Donald Revell, for your guidance and inspiration. And to Christine Marshall for your continuous and loving attention.

"Dear C.—" is for Chris Vargas; "Sent" is for Javanica Curry; "City of Angels" is for Rosy Thowtho; and "A Farmhouse" and "A Wave" are for Christine Marshall.

Barrow Street Poetry

Boy with Flowers
Ely Shipley (2008)

Gold Star Road
Richard Hoffman (2007)

Hidden Sequel
Stan Sanvel Rubin (2006)

Annus Mirabilis
Sally Ball (2005)

A Hat on the Bed
Christine Scanlon (2004)

Hiatus
Evelyn Reilly (2004)

3.14159+
Lois Hirshkowitz (2004)

Selah
Joshua Corey (2003)